Body Parts

جسم کے حصّے

Author: Bushra A
Illustrator: Saima A

THIS BOOK BELONGS TO

Head (Sur)
سر

Hair(Baal)
بال

Ears (Kaan)
کان

Eyes (Ankh)
آنکھ

Mouth(Monh)
منہ

Nose (Naak)
ناک

Teeth (Dant)
دانت

Toung (Zuban)
زبان

Neck(Gurdan)
گردن

Shoulders(Kanday)

Belly (Pait)
پیٹ

Arms (Bazoo)
بازو

Legs(Tangain)
ٹانگیں

Hand (Hath)
ہاتھ

Feet (Paon)
پاؤں

Head
سر
(Sur)

Hair
بال
(Baal)

Ear
کان
(Kaan)

Eye
آنکھ
(Ankh)

Mouth
منہ
(Monh)

Nose
ناک
(Naak)

Teeth
دانت
(Dant)

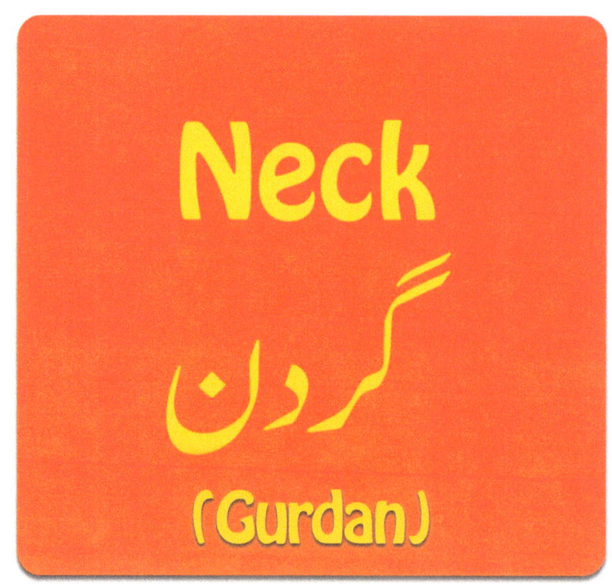
Neck
گردن
(Gurdan)

Shoulders
کندھے
(Kanday)

Belly
پیٹ
(Pait)

Arms
بازو
(Bazo)

Legs
ٹانگیں
(Tangain)

Hands
ہاتھ
(Hath)

Feet
پاؤں
(Paon)

More interesting children's bilingual books

https://www.youtube.com/c/Kahaniclubkidslearning/videos
https://www.facebook.com/kahani.club.58
https://www.instagram.com/clubkahani/

www.ingramcontent.com/pod-product-compliance
Lightning Source LLC
LaVergne TN
LVHW071131160826
845679LV00005B/1243

9798842189847